August - 1989

To Margaret & Peter

Love from
Norm, Tari,
Stacey, Adrienne
& Courtney

CANADA

CAN

This edition published by
W H Smith Publishers, Canada.

Produced by
Bison Books Corp.
15 Sherwood Place
Greenwich, CT 06830
USA

ISBN 0-88665-451-3

Printed in Hong Kong

ADA

KT CATHARINE HALEY

SIGN MIKE ROSE

B. Mitchell

A Bison Book

For Robin, with love

Ulrich Ackermann: 72 bottom, 76-77, 92, 153 bottom, 185 top, 186 both, 187 bottom.

Banff Springs Hotel: 156.

Cyr Color Photo Agency: J D Carmichael 133 top; Murray Jaffe 140 bottom; Charles McNulty 31 bottom; Brenda Purdue 89; Gary Taylor 1.

Darryl T Davies: 20-21, 30, 40, 41 bottom, 48-49, 99, 119, 122 bottom, 192.

Metropolitan Toronto Convention and Visitors Association: 109.

Photo/Graphics Stock Library, Vancouver BC: 55; Carolyn Angus 72 top; Michael E Burch 100, 101, 108, 110-111, 114, 115, 132 bottom, 136, 157, 171 bottom, 172, 174 bottom right, 175, 189 bottom; John Burridge 47, 52-53, 57, 58-59, 85, 141; Fred Chapman 137; Doug Hankin 188; Bob Herger 126, 127, 152, 165, 166, 169; Ralph Klassen 138; J A Kraulis 11, 12-13, 14 top, 16, l7, 18-19, 23, 25, 26-27, 29, 34-35, 37 top, 38-39, 50-51, 54, 61, 66, 69, 73, 74-75, 78, 80-81, 83, 86 both, 90, 93, 95, 96-97, 98, 104-105, 106, 107, 118, 120-l21, 122 top, 123, 125, 130-131, 134-135, 139, 143, 144-145, 146, 147, 149, 158-159, 167, 168, 170, 171 top, 176, 177 top, 180 top, 182-183, 184, 187 top, 190-191; R W Laurilla 84 bottom, 177 bottom; Gar Lunney 14 bottom, 15 bottom, 60, 62, 87 top, 174 bottom left; Gunter Marx 63, 116, 117 top, 168, 178-179, 180 bottom, 181; Vlado Matisic 112-113, 173; Patrick McGinnis 161; Pat Morrow 132 top, 148; Darrell G Noakes 129, 133 bottom; E Otto 102-103; Al Robinson 91 bottom; Jurgen Vogt 15 top, 22, 24, 31 top, 32, 33, 36, 37 bottom, 41 top, 42, 43 top, 44-45 top, 44 bottom, 56, 65, 67, 68, 70-71, 79, 82, 84 top, 87 bottom, 88, 91 top; Terry Willis 162; Richard Wright 43 bottom, 128, 140 top, 154, 185 bottom, 189 top; Cameron Young 150-151, 153 top, 155, 160.

The author and publisher would like to thank Jean Chiaramonte Martin who edited this book and did the picture research.

INTRODUCTION

Canada is the second largest country in the world, with an area of almost four million square miles. It is the entire upper half of North America, except for Alaska and Greenland. Canada's western boundary is the border of Alaska and the Pacific Ocean. To the south lies Canada's only tangential neighbor, the United States, below a border marked by a swath of cut timber and untilled prairie which runs from the Strait of Georgia in British Columbia to Lake of the Woods, Ontario along the 49th Parallel. The border continues east through four of the Great Lakes and up the St Lawrence River. Eventually it reaches its easternmost point where the St Croix River empties into the Bay of Fundy. The eastern border is the Atlantic Ocean, reaching north into the Labrador Sea, Davis Strait (which divides Canada from Greenland) and Baffin Bay. Canada's northern boundary is the Arctic Ocean and the ice-covered islands of the District of Franklin, in the Northwest Territories.

The name Canada is a derivation of the Huron Indian word *kanata* which means a settlement or collection of huts. According to legend it was the reply given to Jacques Cartier when he asked an Indian at the village of Hochelaga where he was. In later years, attempts were made to give the country a different name—Albionara, Norland, Superior, Borealia—but Canada it has remained. To the French, until their great colony was lost, it was always New France.

Today Canada consists of ten provinces and two territories, and within the vast area live approximately 24 million people. About half live in the 25 great metropolitan areas, including Toronto, Montreal, Edmonton and Vancouver. Canada prides itself on having a population that is a mosaic, each group adding to the beauty that is the whole. The largest ethnic group in Canada remains British, except in Quebec where it is French, but Canada is also home to many other nationalities. There are also 300,000 native Indians and Inuit, many of whom live in the remote districts of the Northwest Territories.

About 10,000 years ago, at the end of the last great ice age, the glaciers which had covered most of North America retreated. The action of the ice and rocks had dug great pits and holes in the Precambrian rock that remained. This was the base of the Canadian Shield and the pits and holes became the ponds and lakes of Canada. In the west, the retreating ice left behind Lake Agassiz, a great shallow basin which drained into Hudson Bay. In its place were Lakes Winnipeg and Manitoba and the plain of the Red River, whose rich soil became the prime wheat-growing area in the country. Earlier upheavals in the east, followed by erosion caused by moving ice at the end of the last ice age, formed the Laurentians, while the melting ice had filled the valleys and surrounded outcroppings of land to make the rivers, bays and islands of the Maritime provinces. Similar geologic phenomena had created the sharp cordillera and the high Rockies in the far west.

The first people arrived in Canada some 28,000 years ago by way of a land bridge over the Bering Strait. Following the supply of food, they moved into the Yukon and Northwest Territories, and then south along the corridor of the Rocky Mountains and from there throughout the rest of North and South America. It is believed that the ancestors of the Inuit were the latest arrivals, some 13,000 years ago. The land bridge disappeared with the withdrawal of the last ice age, leaving these paleolithic peoples to develop their own cultures and civilizations.

It has been proven that the Vikings sailed and settled along the eastern coast of Canada around 1000 AD, and that the European fishing fleets were familiar with the Grand Banks by the fifteenth century. The earliest sponsored voyage was that of John Cabot in 1497. Cabot had been commissioned by Henry VII to seek a fast route to the fabled wealth of the Indies. Cabot's first landfall was one where 'The soile is barren in some places, & yeeldeth little fruit, but it is full of white beares, and stagges farre greater than ours. ... [The ocean] yeeldeth plenty of fish ... there is a great abundance of cod.' Cabot sailed further south along the coast which he thought to be Asia, but eventually turned back to England.

The French, too, were seeking a path to the Indies, and their explorers sailed further into the new land. Men like Jacques Cartier and Samuel de Champlain discovered the great river they called the St Lawrence, and took expeditions into the deep forest, finding a land that was fertile, rich and free. Both the English and the French sent parties of colonists to settle the new land. Many of these settlements were wiped out by disease and hunger, but enough succeeded to maintain a

European presence in Canada. The French, in particular, developed a successful culture along the banks of the St Lawrence. The English stayed on the coast, harvesting the riches of the sea, while fur trappers from both countries found great wealth in the native animal pelts.

Eventually the French and English came into conflict, a situation which was aggravated by wars between the two powers on European soil. With the fall of Quebec in 1759, the British took control of North America. Following the rebellion of their southern colonies, British sympathizers moved into the Loyal colonies in the north, increasing the population of the Maritime provinces and Ontario. When the British and their former colonies, now the United States, went to war again in 1812, the Canadians drew together to withstand the attacks and battles along the common frontier.

Throughout the nineteenth century, the fur traders under the auspices of the Hudson's Bay Company and its rival the North West Company continued to explore the vast territory claimed by Canada, opening it to settlement, while the older colonies experimented with self government and eventually banded together to create the Dominion of Canada in 1867. The completion of the transcontinental railroad in 1885 made the vast empty prairies accessible, and many emigrants from Europe joined the westward movement, establishing farms on the great plains. The northern territories attracted new citizens when gold was struck in the Yukon in 1896.

In the twentieth century, Canada has continued to grow. Canadians fought bravely in World War I. The depression of the 1930s did not leave the country untouched, and like many other nations, the Canadian people banded together against fascism in World War II. Canada provided men, planes, weapons and ships for the war in Europe, and Halifax, Nova Scotia was a major gathering point for the ships on the north Atlantic convoy. After the war, Canada opened its shores to the displaced, adding a further leavening to the population. Politically Canada has gained greater independence from the mother country, Great Britain, and become a member of the United Nations. Domestically, there are differences between French-speaking Quebec and the rest of Canada, but a very Canadian spirit of conciliation and compromise ensures the unity of the country.

Enormous natural resources including timber, ore, minerals and hydro-power also work to Canada's advantage. But although Canada's industrial development has kept pace with the twentieth century, it has retained the charm and character of habitant farmers in Quebec, and Maritime fishermen. Its vast size and small population have allowed Canada to remain a country of unsurpassed beauty, from the rocky shores of the east to the majestic Rockies of the West, and from the rich lands of the prairie provinces to the frozen arctic islands of the north.

NEWFOUNDLAND

The story of European exploration and settlement of North America actually begins in Newfoundland, the easternmost province of Canada. In the tenth century, the Vikings, according to traditional sagas, found the places called Markland, Helluland and Vinland, which may have been Newfoundland. Viking remains and the ruins of a settlement at L'Anse Aux Meadows, Newfoundland were discovered in 1961.

The Vikings were followed by the fishing fleets of most of the European maritime powers. When John Cabot anchored in a protected bay on the eastern side of the great island in 1497, and named it St John's for the feast day of the saint, the Basques and the Portuguese had already been there hauling and salting cod. After more than a century of secretive fishing and shipping by merchants and seamen of Bristol and other West Country ports, Sir Humphrey Gilbert claimed the island in the name of Queen Elizabeth in 1583.

For many years thereafter the British discouraged settlements, but individuals continued to live in the small harbours and coves. The first permanent settlement was at Cupids in 1613. The French also made inroads on Newfoundland, and a French force under the Sieur d'Iberville marched across the eastern Avalon peninsula and destroyed the town of St John's in 1697. The Treaty of Utrecht granted the 'newe Founde Lande' to Great Britain in 1713. And over a century later, the government finally legalized colonization.

Newfoundland was England's first colony and it remained so until it became self governing in 1855. The financial problems of the Great Depression led to the suspension of independent government, and the colony was ruled by a commission in England. During World War II the colony served as a base for the north Atlantic convoy, and the development of the great airfields at Gander and Goose Bay led to the post-war opening of the timber and mineral resources of Newfoundland. In 1946 Newfoundlanders were given the choice of remaining under British rule, returning to self government or joining the Dominion of Canada, which they did in 1949.

Newfoundland has two parts, the island of Newfoundland and the mainland territory of Labrador, which is heavily forested and rich in minerals, ore and water power. The isolation of this part of the world has made it difficult for Newfoundland to realize these riches, and most Newfoundlanders still survive by fishing, living in the remote outports or villages as they have for several hundred years. Many of the outports can still only be reached by boat, and this isolation has preserved the Newfoundlanders' way of life, including their distinct speech, accent and vocabulary.

The remote beauty of Newfoundland has drawn visitors for many years. A remarkable haven for birds, Newfoundland is the nesting ground for many arctic and sub-arctic species, like gannets, loons, murres, guillemots and puffins. There are two notable National Parks: Gros Morne, on the western side, renowned for the deep fjords that cut between the high cliffs that dominate the coast; and Terra Nova, on the Atlantic coast, which has long, isolated beaches from which can be seen the harp and grey seals, as well as dolphins and killer whales, in Bona Vista Bay. The Avalon Wilderness Area, southwest of St John's, is a fascinating parkland of inland muskeg and ponds. In early summer, small icebergs can be seen drifting down either side of Newfoundland in the Labrador current, a visible reminder of the northern situation of this land of rugged beauty.

11   Upturned fishing boats rest outside the church at Gander Bay, Newfoundland.

12/13   On Fogo Island, off the northern coast of Newfoundland, fishermen bring the day's catch ashore at twilight.

14 top   The docks on New World Island in *Newfoundland are built of wooden piers filled with stone ballast. Lobster traps are stacked on the hill behind the boathouses.*

14 bottom   The cold Labrador current brings *small ice floes down either side of Newfoundland. At the Change Islands, near Fogo, they drift among the fishing boats at anchor.*

15 top   Fishermen band together to haul out the boats in this remote fishing outport at Bay de Verde, Newfoundland.

15 bottom   The rich waters of the Grand Banks are filled with cod, halibut and flounder which fill the boats of fishermen from Harbour Breton, on the sound side of Newfoundland.

16   Beyond the stack of lobster traps, the houses of Triton, a fishing outport on Notre Dame Bay, cling to the rocky Newfoundland coast.

17   The provincial capital of Newfoundland, St John's, was named by explorer John Cabot for the day he discovered it, the feast day of St John, 24 June 1497.

18/19   At South Head, the mouth of the narrows leading to St John's, stands the Fort Amherst lighthouse and the ruins of concrete gun emplacements built to defend the port from U-Boats during World War II.

20/21 Small cruise ships add to the lights that are reflected in the deep water harbour of St John's.

22 The brightly painted clapboard houses of St John's march down the steep streets to the harbour at the foot of the hill.

23 A garden of multicoloured lupine stands out against the green of a Newfoundland field.

24   Cape Bona Vista, on the eastern coast
of Newfoundland, is a popular nesting place
of gannets, terns and many species of gull.

25   Black backed murres, which look like
small penguins, live in colonies on the rocky
cliffs of Newfoundland.

26/27   Gros Morne National Park, on the
western coast of Newfoundland, is famous for
its deep fjords and the vast number of rare
birds that nest within its boundaries.

PRINCE EDWARD ISLAND AND NEW BRUNSWICK

A Micmac Indian legend says that the God Glooskap painted everything that was beautiful in the world. When he was finished he mixed the remaining colours together and created Abegweit—Prince Edward Island. Discovered by the French explorer Jacques Cartier in 1534, the island was first used by French fishermen for salting fish to preserve it on the long voyage back to France. Samuel de Champlain claimed the island for France in 1603 and named it Ile St Jean, but there was little settlement until the British took over the French possessions following the Treaty of Paris at the end of the Seven Years War in 1763. The name was changed to the Island of St John and the capital became the new settlement named for the wife of George III, Charlotte Town. Originally part of the Nova Scotia colony, Prince Edward Island gained its independence in 1769, at a time when the population was barely 250. New settlers arrived from Scotland, Ireland and England, frequently as tenants of a landowner who remained in England. The name of the island was finally changed to Prince Edward Island in 1799, in honor of Prince Edward, the Duke of Kent and youngest son of George III, who was then commander of the British troops in North America.

Lack of experienced politicians delayed self government until 1851, and subsequent disagreements over land reform and the incursions of the railroads complicated matters. Delegates from the British colonies in North America met in Charlottetown in 1864, a conference which led to Confederation in 1867. After several years of poor economy, Prince Edward Island became the seventh province in 1873. One result of Confederation was the end of tenant farming, as the provincial government bought up the land from the absentee owners and sold it outright to the tenant farmers.

The island, which has been described as 'two huge beaches separated by potato fields' is low-lying except for the sandstone cliffs on the south coast near Charlottetown. For a century it has been a favorite summer resort of Canadians in the eastern provinces because of its peaceful pace and its great beauty. Despite the short growing season, Prince Edward Island is an important agricultural district for vegetables and fruit. Equally well known are the shellfish, especially the oysters from Malpeque Bay, on the north side of the island. Only 140 miles long, and between four and 40 miles wide, Prince Edward Island truly is 'the Garden of the Gulf.'

Across the Northumberland Strait lies the province of New Brunswick, which was also discovered by Cartier in 1534, when he sailed into Chaleur Bay. He described it thus: 'the land along the south side of it [Chaleur Bay] is as fine and as good land, as arable and as full of beautiful fields and meadows as any we have seen.' Claimed by Champlain in 1603, the first settlement was established on St Croix Island, at the mouth of the St Croix River, near the present boundary with the United States. The French encouraged settlement, and farmers came from Brittany to the New World where they augmented their income by fur trapping. While fighting amongst themselves, these settlers occasionally banded together to combat attacks by the colonists in New England.

Under the Treaty of Utrecht in 1713, this area, known as Acadia, was ceded to Great Britain. In 1755, following the British capture of Fort Beausejour, the Acadians were forced to take an oath of allegiance to the British on pain of expulsion. Roughly 8000 Acadians were shipped to other British colonies, or as far away as Louisiana, where they are still known as Cajuns. Within 20 years, many of them had returned, settling along the coast of the Gulf of St Lawrence and Chaleur Bay.

Following the American Revolution, those colonists who had remained loyal to Great Britain emigrated to the remaining British colonies in North America. Many of them settled along the southern coast of New Brunswick, and in the city of St John. In 1784, the area known as Nova Scotia was divided in two, the western side being named New Brunswick for the family name of George III, Brunswick-Luneburg.

The capital of the province is the inland city of Fredericton, named for the second son of George III. Fredericton lies in the heart of the deep forest that makes up most of New Brunswick, the province between the woodland and the sea.

29 The checkerboard fields of Prince Edward Island.

30   Near Victoria, summer cottages line the shore of Northumberland Strait which divides Prince Edward Island from the mainland.

31 top   Cavendish, on the north side of Prince Edward Island, is famous for its great sand dunes and long white beaches.

31 bottom   The great blue heron is a popular resident of the marshes and ponds of Prince Edward Island National Park.

32 Charlottetown, the provincial capital of Prince Edward Island and the cradle of Confederation, is a city of Victorian houses and tree-shaded streets.

33 Towering elms surround the city squares of Fredericton, the provincial capital of New Brunswick.

34/35 Colourful paintwork brightens a church and house on Ile Lameque on the Acadian coast of New Brunswick.

36   The Carlton Martello tower, built during the War of 1812, overlooks the city and harbour of Saint John, New Brunswick.

37 top   Sea mist and sun paint patterns on the rocky shore of New Brunswick's Campobello Island.

37 bottom   Curious rock formations created by wind and tide are found at The Rocks Provincial Park near Hopewell Cape, New Brunswick.

38/39   Trees silhouetted in the evening light near Westmoreland, Prince Edward Island.

40   The island of Grand Manan, on the border of New Brunswick, is the biggest island in the Bay of Fundy and is famous for its lobsters.

41 top   The Kings Landing Historical Settlement recreates life in the colony of New Brunswick from the 1790s to the time of Confederation.

41 bottom   St Andrews by the Sea was founded by Loyalists from Castine, Maine, many of whom brought their houses with them section by section on barges. The tide at St Andrews, as at other towns on the Bay of Fundy, may run to 40 feet or more.

42   Province House in Charlottetown, Prince Edward Island, built in the 1840s, was the site of the conference which led to the Confederation of Nova Scotia, New Brunswick, Ontario and Quebec to form Canada in 1867. Prince Edward Island joined in 1873.

43 top   Seagulls hover above the fishing boats and boathouses of North Rustico, Prince Edward Island.

43 bottom   Green Gables, a farmhouse near Cavendish, was immortalised by Lucy Maude Montgomery, the author of Anne Of Green Gables and many other children's books. It is now a museum.

44   The Saint John dry dock is one of the largest in the world.

44/45   The year-round port of Saint John, New Brunswick, dates back to a fortified trading post established in 1631.

NOVA SCOTIA

Like Newfoundland, Nova Scotia was discovered by John Cabot, who is thought to have come ashore at Cape North on Cape Breton Island as early as 1497. The French attempted several settlements in the early sixteenth century, and there is evidence of a Portuguese colony around the same time. The first permanent settlement in Nova Scotia, and in Canada, was at Port Royal, established by Samuel de Champlain and Pierre de Monts in the Annapolis Basin in 1605. It was here that Champlain founded *L'Ordre de Bon-Temps* (The Order of Good Cheer), a social club created to brighten the first winter in the colony known as Acadia. In 1613 Port Royal was captured and burned by English raiders from Virginia under Captain Samuel Argall. It was one of the first skirmishes of the long conflict that would end with the loss of New France to the British Crown, but the French settlements continued to grow.

In 1621, acting on Cabot's claim of the entire continent for the British, Sir William Alexander, a court favorite of James I, attempted to settle some of his countrymen in the colony he called New Scotland or Nova Scotia. His colony lasted a brief four years, but the name remained. In 1636, the French established a working colony of farm and trading posts that was almost self sufficient. Many of the farmers came from Brittany, a country with a long history of recovering land from the sea, a practice which these Acadians put to use in the Annapolis Basin. Eventually the conflict between England and France overtook them, and they were expelled from their farms during *La Grande Dispersion* in 1755. It is a point of history best known from Longfellow's poem, *Evangeline*. When a number of these Acadians returned, they resettled in the area around Yarmouth, on the Bay of Fundy.

Many of their farms were taken over by Loyalists fleeing the new American Republic, and by the Scots who were being evicted from their Highland homes during the Clearances. They brought with them their language, music and such place names as Inverary, New Glasgow and Caledonia, which make Nova Scotia, with its native heather and thistle, truly New Scotland. The south coast of the island also boasts a strong population of German and Swiss immigrants who became great deep-water fishermen and boat builders. The famous schooner *Bluenose*, which outraced the fastest American sailing ships in the 1920s, was built in the German settlement of Lunenburg.

Nova Scotia was the first colony in British North America to achieve its own government, elected by its own citizens, and was also one of the four colonies that banded together in Confederation in 1867. The provincial capital is the port of Halifax, named for the Earl of Halifax, a government minister to George II who was involved in the city's founding as a military and naval base in 1749. A spectacular harbour, Halifax has also been a centre of maritime shipping since the days when sailing ships carried the flag of Nova Scotia around the world. It was from Halifax that a British army under General Wolfe set out to capture and destroy the great French fortress at Louisbourg. Now rebuilt, the Fort of Louisbourg is only one of the many tourist attractions in Nova Scotia. Around the coast of Cape Breton Island winds the 296-kilometre Cabot Trail, and in the middle lies Bras d'Or Lake, a popular place for sailing and other water sports. Kejimkujik National Park preserves some of the province's finest woodland. But no part of Nova Scotia is more than 35 miles from salt water and like its neighbors, Nova Scotia is still dependent upon the sea.

47   The Bluenose II, a replica of the famous fishing schooner the Bluenose, whose image appears on the Canadian ten-cent piece, was built at Lunenburg, Nova Scotia.

48/49   The Cabot Trail covers 296 kilometres along the spectacular coast of Cape Breton Island.

50/51   A family of scarecrows brightens the roadside along the Cabot Trail in Nova Scotia.

52/53   The Cape Breton Highlands National Park occupies most of northern Cape Breton Island. The salt-sprayed coastal areas are covered with ground juniper and other wild plants such as black crowberry.

54   Sea surge beats against the rocks of Brier Island on the Nova Scotia side of the Bay of Fundy.

55   The tides of the Bay of Fundy have worn smooth the rocks and pebbles on the beach at Tiverton.

56   Bright window boxes and freshly painted clapboards decorate a house in Lunenburg, one of Nova Scotia's great fishing ports, which was originally settled by French, Swiss and German immigrants.

57   The Old Town Clock has been a landmark in Halifax, Nova Scotia since it was built in 1803.

58/59   A traditional star-shaped fortress built in the early nineteenth century, the Citadel at Halifax overlooks the city and the harbour.

60   Gaily coloured fishing floats and lines on board a boat at Clark's Harbour on Cape Sable Island, Nova Scotia.

61   A red boathouse adds brightness to a landscape near Margaree Harbour on Cape Breton Island.

62   Oxen are still used occasionally to plow on small holdings in Nova Scotia.

63   The province's Scottish heritage is celebrated every summer during the Highland Games at Antigonish.

QUEBEC

Quebec, *la belle province*, embodies the lasting heritage of the French empire in the New World. Three hundred and fifty years after its founding and after 200 years as a Gallic island in an English sea, Quebec remains the seat of the French heritage in Canada.

Under the guidance of Samuel de Champlain, the first settlers built a gracious city of stone reminiscent of those they had left behind in France. For the city built on the site of the Indian settlement of Stadcona, Champlain chose the Indian word for a place where the water narrows - *kebec* - and gave it to the new city in 1608. The walled city of Quebec grew rich from the export fur trade and the thriving settlements spread out along the banks of the St Lawrence and smaller rivers. The pattern of these farms, long strips of land with a short stretch on the river, which was the main artery of traffic, is still visible. A number of them are still owned and farmed by descendants of the original *habitants*.

The idyll of New France came to an end with the Battle of Quebec in 1759, when an English force under General James Wolfe stormed the cliffs below the Plains of Abraham and in ten minutes defeated the French defenders under the Marquis de Montcalm. Both Wolfe and Montcalm were killed. The Treaty of Paris in 1763, which marked the end of the Seven Years War in Europe, finally ceded New France to Great Britain.

The French were able to maintain their own identity in part because of the Quebec Act of 1774, which restored French civil law to the areas that had been French colonies. The constitution of 1771 had divided the territory of Quebec into two parts, Lower Canada for the French-speaking area, and Upper Canada for the wilderness recently settled by the United Empire Loyalists. The two were united again in 1841, but separated for the last time at Confederation in 1867. Quebec has continued to maintain her French identity and language in the twentieth century. The *revolution tranquille* created reforms in education as well as a social, economic, cultural and political awakening to the rights of the French-speaking population.

The second great city to be founded in the province was Montreal, built on the site of the Indian town of Hochelaga, on an island where the Ottawa River flows into the St Lawrence. The city took its name from the mountain behind it which Jacques Cartier had named in honor of one of the Medici cardinals who had once been bishop of Monreale, Sicily. In 1642, the trading fort built by Champlain became a mission. In the eighteenth century, it became a centre of the fur trade, and today, it is Canada's second largest city and one of the centres of Canadian finance. The site of the 1967 World Exposition and the Olympics of 1976, Montreal has astonished visitors by its cosmopolitan qualities, its modern subway and its fine restaurants.

North of Quebec City are the Laurentians, among the oldest mountains in the world, renowned for their winter sports, summer fishing and autumn hunting. The Charlevoix region, between the Laurentians and the Saguenay River is called Quebec's Switzerland. It is popular with skiers as well as those who wish to enjoy the small villages which are living monuments to New France.

65 The Montreal skyline is a study in architectural contrasts, from French Colonial to Art Deco and modern international styles.

66 The dome of St Joseph's Oratory in Montreal is illuminated at night.

67 The city of Montreal still has a farmer's market at Maisonneuve, which sells flowers and fresh produce.

68   Modern sculpture decorates the plaza in front of the Esso/BNP Building in Montreal.

69   Colourful tiles and elaborate carvings grace the mansard roofs of the houses along Montreal's Avenue Laval.

70/71   The interior of the Basilica of Notre-Dame was designed by the noted French-Canadian artists Ozias Leduc and Victor Bourgeau. A remarkable example of neo-Gothic architecture, the church contains several stained-glass windows showing the history of early Montreal.

72 top   A farmhouse in a winter landscape in the Eastern Townships, which were settled by Loyalists who came to Canada after the American Revolution.

72 bottom   The colours of early autumn surround this charming house in the Quebec countryside.

73   South of the St Lawrence River, many of the Quebec farms resemble those in nearby Vermont and New York State.

74/75   A quaint church in the village of Riviere-Trois-Pistoles.

76/77   The towers of the Chateau Frontenac, Quebec City's most famous hotel, and the steeple of the Basilica may be seen from the Plains of Abraham.

78 Quebec's founder, Samuel de Champlain, is honoured by statues throughout the city and the province.

79 The St Lawrence River has made the city of Quebec an important seaport since the seventeenth century.

80/81 Within the walled city of Quebec are found many seventeenth and eighteenth century buildings which are now famous restaurants and museums.

82 The festive season is crowned with Christmas lights at Place Ville Marie in downtown Montreal.

83 Emigrants from the Caribbean celebrate with a carnival during the summer.

84 top   Residents and visitors alike can enjoy many unique restaurants in Old Montreal.

84 bottom   Ice fishing on the frozen lakes and rivers of Quebec is a popular winter sport.

85   A street musician entertains in Old Montreal.

86 top Soccer is played in the Olympic Stadium in Montreal.

86 bottom Winter sports include a cross-country skiing marathon held near Montebello.

87 top The lakes of Quebec, like Lac Quimet, north of Montreal, are perfect for small sailboats.

87 bottom A group of boys engages in an impromptu game of hockey.

88 *The splendour of a Canadian fall can be seen here on a country road near Riviere du Loup.*

89 *The raccoon can find a home wherever there is water and trees.*

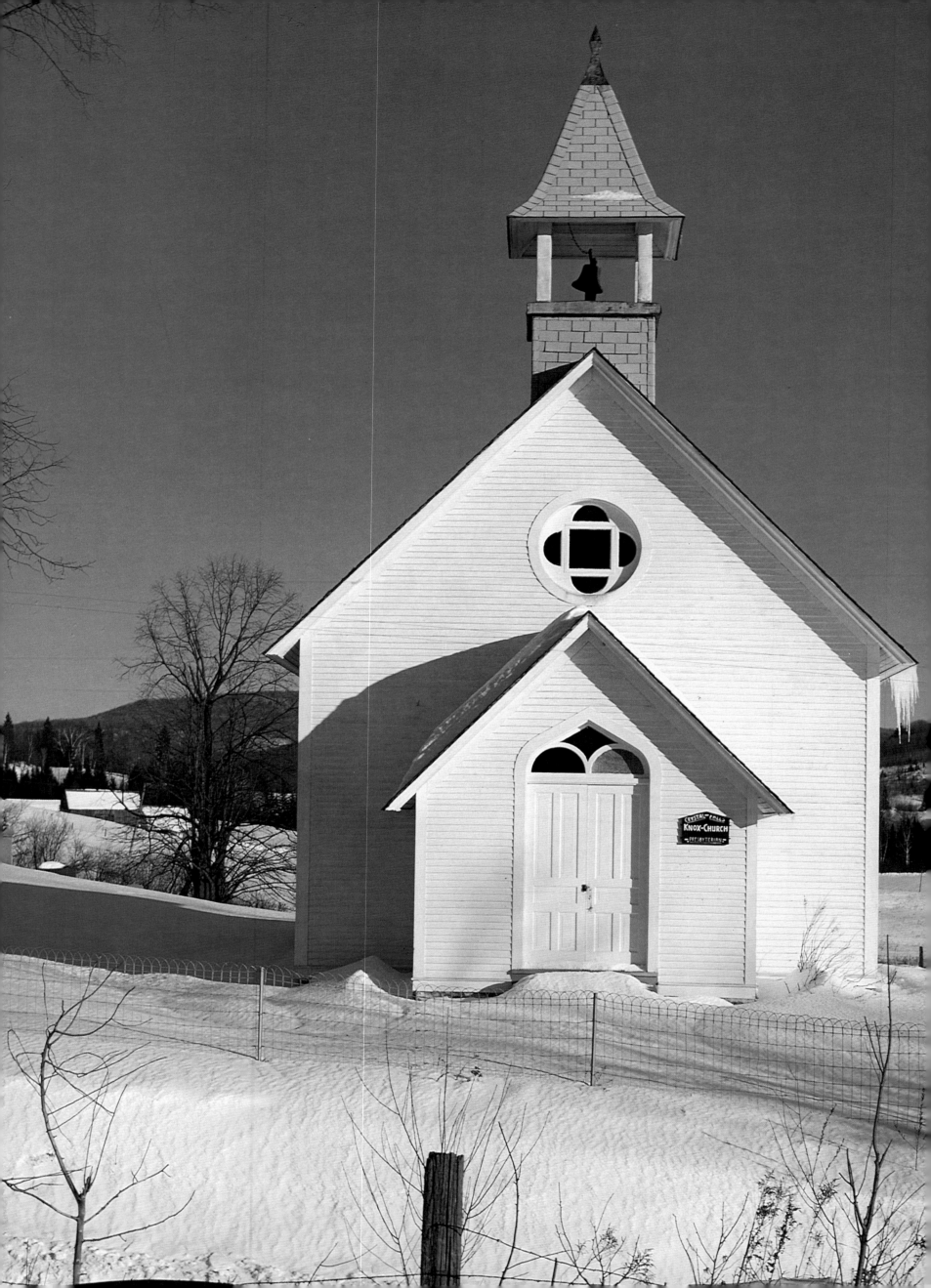

90   A picturesque church in the Rouge River Valley in the Laurentian region, north of Montreal.

91 top   Ice sculptures are a part of many of the winter festivals held at the resorts and villages of the Laurentians.

91 bottom   Gatineau Park, north of Ottawa, the federal capital of Canada, is a popular recreation area with over 97 kilometres of trails for cross-country skiers and snowshoers in winter.

92   The many lakes and rivers of Quebec are ideal for fishing and canoeing.

93   Perce Rock, a limestone rock off the Gaspe Peninsula, was named by Samuel de Champlain. The nearby fishing village has become a resort popular with tourists.

ONTARIO

The province of Ontario is as English as Quebec is French. It is a province of rich farms, timberland and tundra, as well as the thousands of lakes that give the province its name, from an Iroquois Indian word meaning 'shining water.' The second largest province, Ontario was virtually unsettled before 1763. French missionaries had established outposts in the 1630s, working with the Indians at the Jesuit mission of St Marie Among The Hurons, but the primary settlement began after the American Revolution, when the United Empire Loyalists settled along the upper reaches of the St Lawrence and Niagara rivers. It was part of the colony of Quebec until 1791, when it was then divided into Upper and Lower Canada. During the war of 1812, the loyalty of the settlers was strengthened as they proved themselves by fighting against the Americans at the battles of Lake Erie and Queenston and suffering a humiliating defeat at Kingston, as well as the burning of York.

After the war, immigration increased as settlers moved west from the Maritimes and others came from the British Isles. By 1837, the people of Ontario wanted a say in the government, resenting the power held by the earlier settlers known as the Family Compact, who were connected by marriage and business ties. The rebellion, in which the majority sought reform within the framework of British institutions, was unsuccessful, but their dissatisfaction brought about a change of government in 1841. Once again united with the province of Quebec, the two provinces whose cultures continued to clash were divided again at the time of Confederation, and Upper Canada became Ontario.

Within the boundaries of the province great cities began to grow, including the provincial capital of Toronto on the shores of Lake Ontario, now one of the most cosmopolitan cities in Canada. The federal capital at Ottawa, across the river from Hull, Quebec, began as the canal terminus of Bytown. It is now a city of parks and gardens, as well as politicians.

Ontario is the most populous province, with major centres such as Windsor, Kingston, and Thunder Bay, the great grain port on Lake Superior. It is also the most highly industrialized, with great steel mills at Hamilton and Sault Ste Marie, as well as mining and smelting areas around Sudbury. But Ontario also contains the largest number of occupied farms, many of them owned by Mennonites, who began settling in Canada in the eighteenth century and continue to run their farms with horse power. Ontario borders four of the Great Lakes—Superior, Huron, Erie and Ontario—and thus is part of the great shipping system that brings grain out of the west, as well as cars from Windsor and ore from Thunder Bay.

To the north lies the vast forest of central Canada and above that the treeless tundra, for Ontario reaches as far north as Hudson Bay. Ontario also boasts the southernmost point in Canada, a promontory of land extending into Lake Erie. Many nature preserves, from Polar Bear Provincial Park in the north, to great wilderness areas, like Algonquin Provincial Park, north of Toronto, and to Point Pelee, best known as a migratory rest for the monarch butterflies who swarm there in early fall, are proof of the great diversity of Ontario.

95 A boathouse on Lake Muskoka, a popular summer resort in Ontario.

96/97 A peaceful summer scene on a farm near Precious Corners, Ontario.

98   Rows of seedlings contrast with the dark earth of Holland Marsh in Ontario.

99   The drive to the Ontario Experimental Farm near Ottawa is lined with maples and other deciduous trees.

100   The province of Ontario has shoreline along four of the Great Lakes.

101 The Maid of the Mist, one of a fleet of tourist boats, brings visitors to Niagara to the foot of Horseshoe Falls.

102/103 Goat Island lies on the Canadian side of the Niagara border between the American Falls and Horseshoe Falls.

104/105 Ontario Place, in the harbour at Toronto, is a marina and water amusement park, with theatres and cafes.

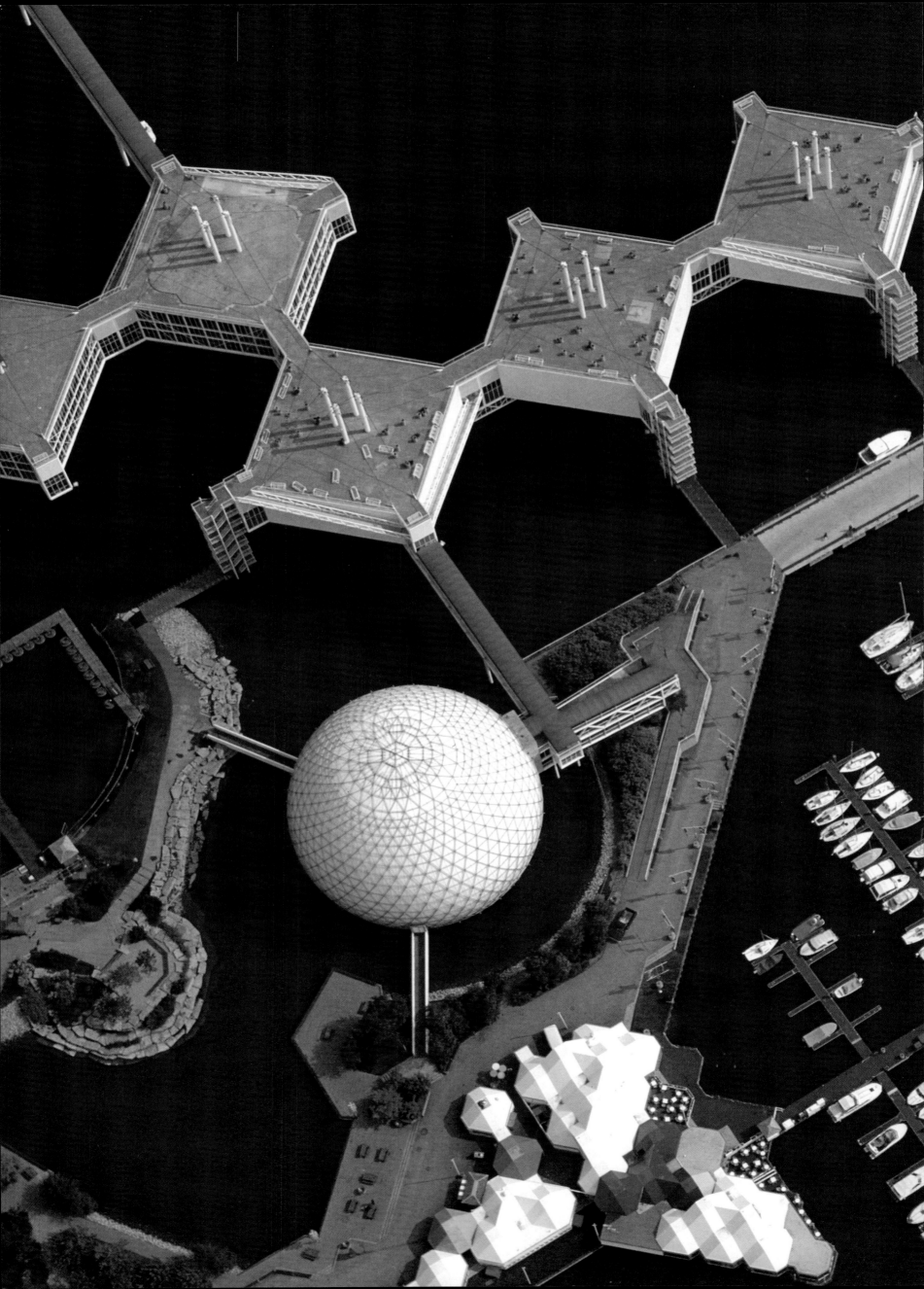

106 *The CN Tower, the tallest free-standing structure in the world, rises above the city of Toronto.*

107 *Illuminations on the Old City Hall of Toronto are reflected in the pool in front of the New City Hall.*

108 Running between Dundas and Queen streets in Toronto is the Eaton Centre, a three-level complex of restaurants and shops.

109 The New City Hall of Toronto was designed by Viljo Revell, a Finnish architect. It consists of two curved towers encircling the domed city council chambers.

110/111 The Victorian Gothic Parliament Buildings, including the tall carillon known as the Peace Tower, dominate Ottawa's skyline.

112/113 Fresh flowers are sold at the Byward Market in the heart of Ottawa, near the Chateau Laurier, a famous hotel.

114 The Allan MacPherson House in Napanee, Ontario, was built by one of the Loyalists who arrived in the area in 1784. The beehive oven is visible on one side of the main kitchen fireplace.

115   St Mark's Anglican Church in Niagara-on-the-Lake is one of Canada's oldest Anglican churches. Completed in 1810, it was used as a hospital during the War of 1812.

116   Holiday-makers are reflected in a tuba in an oompah band. Oktoberfest celebrates the German heritage of the town of Kitchener, which was known as Berlin until World War I.

117 top   Members of the Royal Canadian Mounted Police perform their celebrated Musical Ride.

117 bottom   Mennonite girls wear the traditional simple clothes of the sect, without buttons or trim.

118 A field of trilliums. The three-petalled wildflower is one of the symbols of the province of Ontario.

119 Along the Rideau Canal in Ottawa great stands of tulips bloom, a present from the Dutch people in thanks for the sanctuary given to the Dutch Royal Family by Canada during World War II.

120/121 Hot air balloons rise above Barrie, Ontario, near Lake Simcoe.

122   top   Colourful autumn leaves float on Ontario's Lake Muskoka.

122   bottom   A brightly painted dinghy, tied up at Chaffey's Locks, is typical of the small craft owned by many Ontarians for fishing.

123   The rich constant green of a spruce contrasts with the red, yellow and orange of autumn leaves on a road near Muskoka, Ontario.

MANITOBA AND SASKATCHEWAN

The prairie provinces of Manitoba and Saskatchewan were once the home of five major Indian tribes, the Chipewyan, the Plains Cree, the Woods Cree, the Assiniboine and the Chippewa. The first white man to set foot in what is today Manitoba was Sir Thomas Button, who came ashore from Hudson Bay in 1612 while searching for Henry Hudson and the Northwest Passage. Button claimed the territory in the name of King James I.

In 1670 Charles II granted trading rights in the territory to the newly established Hudson's Bay Company, and the country became known as Rupert's Land in honor of the King's cousin, Prince Rupert of the Rhine. The trading posts the Hudson's Bay Company set up throughout the territory brought more trappers and explorers into the territory. One of these was Henry Kelsey who in 1690 became the first white man in Saskatchewan. The traders intermarried with the Indians, and their children, known as Metis, in turn became trappers.

Rivalry between the Hudson's Bay Company and its competitor, the North West Company, was intensified by the arrival of settlers in the fertile valleys of the Red and Assiniboine rivers. In 1870, after Confederation, Canada acquired Rupert's Land, 1.5 million square miles, from the Hudson's Bay Company, for $1.5 million. Also that year the tiny province of Manitoba, which at the time was only the settled area around the Hudson's Bay Company fort at Winnipeg, joined Confederation.

The western boundary of Manitoba was extended to the present line in 1881 and the completion of the transcontinental railroad eased the export of wheat, for which the area was already well-known, and the arrival of settlers. Many of these came from the grain-growing areas of the Ukraine and Russia, and they brought with them their religion, customs and architecture.

Saskatchewan, named for the long river that flows within it, was also part of Rupert's Land, and like Manitoba was dotted with the fur trading forts of the Hudson's Bay and North West Companies. The first settlement was on Cumberland Lake in 1774, but settlement did not start in earnest until the time of Confederation, and it was the completion of the transcontinental railroad in 1885 that truly opened the territory. The influx of settlers was pushing the long-established Metis to one side, ignoring their customs and rights. A rebellion ended with the death of their leader Louis Riel, but the Metis were granted some sovereignty by the government in Ottawa.

The capital of Saskatchewan is the city of Regina, named for Queen Victoria by her daughter, the wife of the Governor General. It was the capital of the Northwest Territories until 1905, when Saskatchewan achieved provincial status. It was also the original headquarters of the Royal Canadian Mounted Police, who still have their training depot in Regina.

125 Many immigrants to the prairie provinces came from Russia and the Ukraine. Their distinctive churches can be found throughout Manitoba and Saskatchewan.

126/127 Saskatoon, the second largest city in Saskatchewan, began as a temperance colony on the South Saskatchewan River.

128   The town of Moose Jaw, Saskatchewan, takes its name from the bend of the Moose Jaw River, where the city stands.

129   The Doukhobour Museum at Veregin, Saskatchewan, tells the history of the Doukhobours, a sect which emigrated from Russia at the turn of the century and whose members still inhabit the area.

130/131   The land west of Winnipeg, Manitoba, is some of the most fertile farmland in North America.

132 top Farmers in the prairie provinces make most of their income from grain, including wheat, oats and barley.

132 bottom Fields of sunflowers, which are grown for oil, are a familiar sight during the late summer in Manitoba.

133 top A combine at work harvesting part
of the vast wheat crop of Saskatchewan.

133 bottom The storage of enough fodder
and grain to feed the stock is a necessity in
the long prairie winter.

134/135 *Patterns are created by threshing machines moving around rocky outcrops west of Regina, Saskatchewan.*

136 *Prairie light reflects from the side of a grain elevator in the prosperous southern Manitoba town of Altona.*

137 *The grain elevators have been called the Cathedrals of the West.*

138   At the end of the last ice age, retreating glaciers carved out many lakes and ponds which have become popular fishing spots, particularly in the northern parts of the prairie provinces.

139   The Trans-Canada Highway, completed in 1962, passes by remote farms through Saskatchewan.

140 top   The black-tailed prairie dog, which once lived in enormous colonies in the province, is now only found in a protected area east of Val Marie, Saskatchewan.

140 bottom   The jack rabbit, known by its tremendous ears and great feet, is found throughout the western provinces.

141   Polar bears seek food close to the town of Churchill, Manitoba, near Hudson Bay.

ALBERTA

The third prairie province, Alberta was named for Princess Louise Caroline Alberta, the Marchioness of Lorne and wife of the Governor General who held office from 1878 to 1883. Alberta was also part of the land grant to the Hudson's Bay Company, which was acquired by the Dominion of Canada in 1870. It was first explored by Anthony Enday of the Hudson's Bay Company who was sent to promote trade among the Blackfoot Indians in 1754. The traders of the North West Company also built forts in the territory. As early as 1778 there was one as far north as Lake Athabaska, and Fort Chipewyan, from which Alexander Mackenzie began his long expedition to the Beaufort Sea, was built in 1788. Throughout the nineteenth century, there was a trickle of settlers, mostly traders and Metis, as well as Roman Catholic and Methodist missionaries. The North West Mounted Police established a series of forts on the prairie beginning with Fort McLeod in 1874. The following year they established the one-man post which became the city of Calgary. Once again it was the arrival of the railroad which opened the territory to settlers. In 1904, a strain of early-ripening wheat made grain a more viable product, and more land became available. The territory became a province in 1905.

Though considered a prairie province, the most striking part of Alberta is its western edge, the Rockies. West of Calgary, the rolling grasslands give way to the foothills and then the Rockies themselves. The high peaks are a rugged wilderness, much of it accessible only to the sure-footed mountain goat and the great hawks. Canada's first national park, Banff, is renowned for its marvellous hot springs and excellent skiing. Another remarkable Rocky Mountain park is Jasper, on the British Columbia border, which contains ancient glaciers that feed the emerald green lakes. Other natural wonders of Alberta include Kananaskis Provincial Park, which is known for its canyons and alpine tundra and Dinosaur Provincial Park, with its extensive fossil remains.

The capital of Alberta is Edmonton, the most northern of Canada's major cities. Originally a Hudson's Bay Company fort, Edmonton expanded when the railway spur reached it in 1891. It also became a supply base for the Klondike Gold Rush in 1898. The discovery of oil nearby brought Edmonton into the twentieth century and to its position as a modern vibrant city.

143 Jasper National Park, straddling the border of Alberta and British Columbia, has been a National Park since 1907. The beautiful Tonquin Valley is a favorite spot in the park.

144/145 Edmonton, the capital of Alberta, began as a trading post of the Hudson's Bay Company, and is now a thriving modern city thanks to the discovery of oil.

146 The North Saskatchewan River flows through the city of Edmonton. Its banks are now a series of parks and golf courses.

147 The West Edmonton Mall houses a massive pool, water slides and an ice skating rink as well as over 800 retail shops.

148 Oil rigs, including small 'grasshoppers,' can be seen all around Edmonton.

149 The rolling foothills of the Rockies, west of Calgary, are still part of Canada's grain belt.

150/151 The Calgary Tower in the middle of the city offers views of the Rockies and the Saddledome, a 1988 Olympics venue and home ice for the Calgary Flames of the National Hockey League.

152   Trail riding is popular in Paradise Valley, Banff National Park.

153 top   A highlight of the annual Calgary Stampede is the chuckwagon race.

153 bottom   Members of many of the local Indian tribes, like the Cree and the Blackfoot, gather at dance meetings southwest of Calgary.

154 The giant Pysanka, or Easter Egg, at Vegreville, Alberta, honors the Ukrainian pioneers who settled the area east of Edmonton.

155 Replicas of the area's earlier inhabitants can be seen at the Prehistoric Park in the Calgary Zoo.

156   The Banff Springs Hotel, near the Bow River, stands in a green valley high in the Rocky Mountains.

157   Lake Louise, in Banff National Park, is fed by the Victoria Glacier.

158/159   Moraine Lake, in the Valley of the Ten Peaks, is another popular attraction in Banff National Park.

160 Whitewater rafting can be an exciting experience in the rugged wilderness of Kananaskis Provincial Park.

161 The Colin Range of the Canadian Rockies in Jasper National Park is a popular place for hiking, even in the snow.

162　The black bear is plentiful in the national parks in the Canadian Rockies.

163　Bison graze in the upland meadows of Waterton Lakes National Park.

BRITISH COLUMBIA

The Pacific province of British Columbia is divided from the rest of Canada by the steep Rocky Mountains, and consequently, has always looked west. The coastal area, originally populated by the Indian tribes known as the Vikings of the Pacific for their sailing exploits, was explored by the English Captain James Cook as early as 1778, while he was searching for the Northwest Passage. With the aid of Indian tribes like the Salish, Haida and Kwakiutl, the British established a flourishing fur trade in the area. The growth of this trade alarmed both the Spanish in California and the Russians to the north.

In 1792, Captain George Vancouver circumnavigated the island that bears his name while surveying the Pacific coast from California to Alaska. The first man to reach the coast from the east was Sir Alexander Mackenzie in 1793. He was followed by the North West Company trader, Simon Fraser, who followed the river which bears his name, while establishing trading posts in the Rockies. Fort Victoria, on the southern tip of Vancouver Island, was established in 1843 to secure the British claim to the fur trade. A border conflict with the United States was settled in 1846, and Vancouver Island became a colony in 1849.

The discovery of gold in the Fraser River brought prospectors to the area. Many of these stayed behind to farm, and the British government created a new colony, British Columbia, which was amalgamated with Vancouver Island in 1866. The colony joined Confederation as British Columbia in 1871. One of the terms of Confederation was the building of a transcontinental railroad to join the new province with the east. It remained a major pipeline for the goods and produce of British Columbia until the present. However, it was the building of the Panama Canal in 1915 which brought the coastal city of Vancouver to its present position as a major Pacific port. Vancouver enjoys one of the most beautiful settings in the world. Backed by the rugged Coast Mountains, it is said that you can ski in the morning and sail in the afternoon if you live in Vancouver.

The rise of Vancouver as a trading center left Fort Victoria behind. Now called Victoria, the small city has been the provincial capital of British Columbia for over a century. Victoria enjoys the gentlest climate in all of Canada, and for that reason is chosen by many Canadians and those in the British colonial service for retirement.

165 Butchart Gardens, north of Victoria, British Columbia, were originally planted within an old limestone quarry.

166   A fishing boat on the Cloyoquot Sound returns at twilight to Meares Island, British Columbia.

167   Tidal rock pools like this one at Cape Scott, British Columbia, hold small crabs, sea urchins and seaweed as well as many other varieties of marine life.

168 The Queen Charlotte Islands, off the coast of northern British Columbia, are lushly forested and carpeted with many types of moss.

169 Giant red cedar trees tower over small spruces near Port Renfrew.

170 Colourful alpine wildflowers can be found at high elevations in the Bugaboo Mountains.

171 top   A house sits on the edge of Fraser Canyon.

171 bottom Apple trees bloom in the orchards near Keremeos in southern British Columbia.

172   The Vancouver skyline is silhouetted
against the Coast Mountains.

173   Vancouver's downtown buildings, seen
here from Lost Lagoon in Stanley Park.

174 top   Dancers in Vancouver's Chinatown, the second largest in North America, celebrate the Chinese New Year.

174 bottom left   Vancouver's beautiful setting has attracted many artists.

174 bottom right   Just across Burrard Inlet from Vancouver, the Grouse, Seymour and Cypress mountains offer day and night skiing to young and old alike.

175   The Lion's Gate Bridge over Burrard Inlet connects Vancouver to North and West Vancouver.

176 Sunburst Lake in Mount Assiniboine Provincial Park, in the Canadian Rockies.

177 top Also in the Rockies, Yoho National Park offers shelters for cross-country skiers in the shadow of the Cathedral Mountains.

177 bottom Climbers on Mount Huber, one of the 30 mountains in Yoho National Park over 3000 metres high.

178/179 The Parliament Buildings in Victoria, built in 1898, are illuminated at night.

180 top   A longhouse decorated in the traditional Haida manner, in the Queen Charlotte Islands.

180 bottom   Indian fishermen catch salmon on the Bulkley River at Moricetown, using the traditional long spear.

181   An Indian girl of the Pacific coast wearing traditional dress. Today only three per cent of British Columbia's population is Indian.

THE YUKON AND NORTHWEST TERRITORIES

Despite their isolation, the northern territories of Canada were known, if not fully explored, before the prairie provinces. Many explorers of the sixteenth and seventeenth centuries sought to find the fabled Northwest Passage by sailing through the icebound islands of the north. The traders of the Hudson's Bay Company and the North West Company also made their way to this land of muskeg, lakes and ice. In 1789, Alexander Mackenzie made his way from Fort Chipewyan to Great Slave Lake, and north along the river that bears his name to the Beaufort Sea in the Arctic.

Mackenzie also gave his name to one of the three districts that now make up the Northwest Territories. The one to the east, Keewatin, is the land of the Inuit, and of the caribou, polar bear and seals that they hunt. The most northern district is Franklin, named for the explorer who disappeared while searching for the Northwest Passage in 1847. It is made up of the northern islands of Baffin Bay. The District of Mackenzie lies between Keewatin and the border with Alaska. The capital of the Northwest Territories is Yellowknife, which was established as recently as 1935 as a gold mining town.

The fourth district of the Northwest Territories was the Yukon, which became a separate territory following the Gold Rush. In 1896 James Carmack and two Indians, Skookum Jim and Tagish Charlie, struck gold in Bonanza Creek near Dawson. The resulting Gold Rush lasted for two years, bringing thousands of people into the territory over the forbidding Chilkoot Pass. Most would leave penniless, but many decided to stay, caught by the beauty and solitude of life in the great north.

The name Yukon comes from a Chilkat word meaning 'the river'. Its capital is Whitehorse, which was a stopping place for the Klondike prospectors. Today the bulk of the Yukon's population of 25,000 lives near Whitehorse, but many still seek the solitude that has always attracted people to the northern reaches, where there is no sun for half the year, but where one is always aware of the north—quiet, solitary and secretive.

183   The Mackenzie River flows north from the Great Slave Lake in the Northwest Territories to empty into the Beaufort Sea. The ponds at the delta are formed by thawing which occurs in the brief summer sun.

184   Kluane National Park in the Yukon is known for the many tall mountains in the St Elias Range.

185 top   Even in summer, snow-capped peaks rise behind Emerald Lake in the Yukon.

185 bottom   Rafting on the South Nahanni River in Nahanni National Park, Northwest Territories. The early explorers used the rivers and lakes of the area in their search for the Northwest Passage.

186 top Near Dezedeasch Lake in the Yukon, a trapper has surrounded his cabin with several cords of wood for the winter.

186 bottom Although dog teams have mostly given way to snowmobiles, a husky puppy is still a valued companion.

187 top   The Downtown Hotel is one of the reminders of Dawson's past as the 'City of Gold' during the Gold Rush of 1897-98.

187 bottom   Sternwheelers like the Tutshi, *now beached at Carcross in the Yukon, once brought supplies to the gold rush towns.*

188   *A female polar bear and her yearling cub cross the ice on the Beaufort Sea.*

189 top   *The grizzly bear is found throughout the northern territories below the treeline.*

189 bottom   *A snowy owl perches on the ground in open country. Its pale plumage is camouflage against the Arctic snow.*

190/191   *A view to the Arctic, as seen through an iceberg from Pang Nirtung on Baffin Island in the Northwest Territories.*